THE LITTLE SCHOOL

THE LITTLE SCHOOL:
Tales of Disappearance & Survival in Argentina

Alicia Partnoy

Translated by Alicia Partnoy
with Lois Athey and Sandra Braunstein

Illustrated by Raquel Partnoy

CLEIS PRESS

Published in the United States by Cleis Press, P.O. Box 8933, Pittsburgh, PA 15221 and P.O. Box 14684, San Francisco, CA 94114.

First Edition.
10 9 8 7 6 5 4 3
Printed in the United States.
ISBN: 0-939416-07-7 paper
ISBN: 0-939416-08-5 cloth
Library of Congress Catalog Card Number: 85-073522
Typesetting: Norm Littlejohn, La Raza Graphics, San Francisco
Cover design: Pete Ivey
Chapter heads motif: Juana Alicia
Interior book design: Astrid Raffin-Peyloz

This book is available on tape to disabled women from the Womyn's Braille Press, P.O. Box 8475, Minneapolis, MN 55408.

Included in these pages is information from the author's testimony on human rights violations in Argentina, which appears in *The Breaking of Bodies and Minds: Torture, Psychiatric Abuse, and the Health Professions,* edited by E. Stover and E. Nightingale, American Association for the Advancement of Science, Freeman & Co. Press, 1985. Map of The Little School from *The Breaking of Bodies and Minds,* used by permission of the artist, Holly Bishop, and the publisher.

In memory
of Daniel, my brother,
for whom life became
so absurd that he
decided to take his own.

Contents

Contents

Preface

Alicia Partnoy has a soft quiet voice that screams. It was the voice I heard when we shared the stage at Sisterfire 1984 and she gave us her poem—a poem Sweet Honey now sings:

They cut off my voice
so I grew two voices
into different tongues
my songs I pour
They cut off my voice
so I grew two voices
in two different tongues
my songs I pour
They took away my sun
two brand new suns
like resplendent drums I am playing —
Today I am playing

I remember feeling I knew who she was when I heard her soft voice screaming—It gave me comfort, made me know once more that I had company.

And now here she is again, giving me her words in a soft quiet voice that shouts and cries and shakes me. This time she gives me words I can walk on to go where she found her nose—and again I am comforted because we have company. It is always good to reach out and find you are not alone.

Yes, they really do take us away and they torture us and they steal our children and kill our sisters and beat our brothers—and the pain of her screaming words cuts off my breath. Then inside the pain—while I am still too scared to breathe—Alicia Partnoy giggles:

The Little School is a long soft freedom love song about having company and surviving.

Bernice Johnson Reagon
Washington D.C.
January 1986

Introduction

n the summer of 1984, after four and a half years in exile, I returned to my homeland to mourn my friends who had disappeared or were killed by the military, to mourn the members of my family who had died during my ordeal of seven years in prison and banishment, and to suffer at the sight of my country ruined after years of dictatorship.

Almost 30,000 Argentines "disappeared" between 1976 and 1979, the most oppressive years of the military rule.

Military coups have not been rare events in the history of my country. In fact, I was born in 1955, the year of the coup that overthrew Juan Peron. A succession of military and short-lived civilian governments followed. It was not until I turned seventeen that Peronists were permitted to participate in Argentina's political life. The Peronist party won the elections. How could a teenager who had never heard anything positive about Peronism from teachers or from the censored media get strongly involved in the movement? My "conversion," as well as that of thousands of youth who had not come from Peronist families, was a gradual process. I grew up loving my country and its people and hating injustice. I did not have many doubts left when I learned that Peronism had given power to the workers by organizing them in strong unions; had improved the living conditions of people through fair wages, retirement plans, vacations, and a good public health system; and had granted women the right to vote. I also learned about the work of Evita, Peron's wife, who was responsible for many of these gains. I knew that Peronism was a very broad movement and that under the umbrella of economic independence, political sovereignty and social justice, there was room for all ideologies. However, like most of the younger generation, I thought that the movement bore the seeds of change to socialism.

At my home town university in Bahía Blanca, I began to get involved. Our main goal was to change the concept of universities as "islands" for scholars who were not concerned with the country's reality. As a student, I worked with others to create programs that would meet what we perceived to be the needs of the Argentine people. I was elected student government representative and was active in the Peronist Youth Movement (*Juventud Universitaria Peronista*). One of my closest friends, Zulma "Vasca" Izurieta, who like myself majored in Literature, worked in a literacy campaign in one of the city's shanty towns. Some of my best friends were Christians who advocated Liberation Theology. The names of most of them are on lists of those who disappeared at the Little School.

By 1975, Peron had died, and Isabel, his third wife and Vice President, was left in charge. Unlike Evita, Isabel did not truly represent the interests of the workers. Furthermore, she handed over control of the repressive apparatus to the military. The youth movement was attacked as a threat to our country's security. Paramilitary groups kidnapped and killed political activists with the support of the police. At the same time the Montoneros, an urban guerrilla movement within Peronism, targeted members of the Armed Forces and big factory owners who were not complying with their workers' demands. The Revolutionary People's Party (ERP), the second largest guerrilla movement, aimed at the same targets.

Finally, in March 1976, the military—along with the national oligarchy and backed by multinational corporations—launched a coup. The new junta heavily censored the media and annulled the constitution. They felt that this was the only way to control not only the youth but also the workers, whose demands for better wages and whose continuous strikes were getting out of hand.

Attending school became hazardous. I had to pass between two soldiers who were sitting with machine guns at the entrance of the building. A highly ranked officer would request my I.D., check it against a list of "wanted" activists and search my belongings. I did not know when my name was going to appear on that list. I stopped going to classes. But the coup triggered my rage, and I decided to become more militant. That decision meant risking my life. My daughter, Ruth, was nine months old. My answer to my own fears was that I had to work for a better society for the sake of my child's future. For almost a year I did so. I clandestinely reproduced and distributed information on the economic situation, the workers' strikes, and the repression.

I learned about "disappearance": the kidnapping of an individual followed by torture and secret detention, which meant that the military denied the fact that the prisoner was in their hands. I did not know that very soon I would become a disappeared person.

On January 12, 1977, at noon, I was detained by uniformed Army personnel at my home, Canadá Street 240, Apt. 2, Bahía Blanca; minutes later the same military personnel detained my husband at his place of work. I was taken to the headquarters of the 5th Army Corps and from there to a concentration camp, which the military ironically named the Little School *(La Escuelita)*. We had no knowledge of the fate of Ruth, our daughter. From that moment on, for the next five months, my husband and I became two more names on the endless list of disappeared people.

The old house of the Little School was located behind the headquarters of the 5th Army Corps, fifteen blocks from the You and I Motel *(Tú y Yo)* on Carrindanga Road, a beltway. The house was near a railroad; one could hear trains, the shots fired at the army command's firing range, and the mooing of cows. I stepped off the Army truck, handcuffed and blindfolded, and by tilting my head, was able to read on the face of the house the letters A.A.A., which stood for *Alianza Anticomunista Argentina*, the name of a parapolice group with whom the military has since denied any relation.

In the Little School there were two rooms where an average of fifteen prisoners remained prone, our hands bound. The floors were wood, the walls yellowing with high windows and dark green shutters and Colonial wrought iron bars. Separating these rooms was a tiled hall where the presence of a guard insured that we neither moved nor spoke. At the end of the hall were the guards' room, a kitchen and a bathroom. A door opened on the patio, where the "torture room," latrine and water tank were located. There was also a trailer where the guards slept; and later they added one or two trailers for more "disappeared" people.

When it rained, the water streamed into the rooms and soaked us. When the temperature fell below zero, we were covered with only dirty blankets; when the heat was unbearable, we were obligated to blanket even our heads. We were forced to remain silent and prone, often immobile or face down for many hours, our eyes blindfolded and our wrists tightly bound.

Lunch was at 1:00 P.M. and dinner at 7:00 P.M.; we went without food for eighteen consecutive hours daily. We were constantly hungry. I lost 20 pounds, going down to 95 pounds (I am 5 ft. 5 in.). Added to the meager food, the lack of sugar or fruits, was the constant state of stress that made our bodies consume calories rapidly. We ate our meals blindfolded, sitting on the bed, plate in lap. When we had soup or watery stew, the blows were constant because the guards insisted that we keep our plates straight. When we were thirsty, we asked for water, receiving only threats or blows in response. For talking, we were punished with blows from a billy jack, punches, or removal of our mattresses. The atmosphere of violence was constant. The guards put guns to our heads or mouths and pretended to pull the trigger.

On April 25, after three and a half months, the guards told me they were taking me "to see how the radishes grow" — a euphemism for death and burial. Instead, I was transferred from the Little School to another place where I remained disappeared for fifty-two more days. The living conditions were better: no blindfold, no blows, better food, a clean cell, daily showers. The isolation was complete and the risk of being killed the same. By June, 1977, my family was informed of my whereabouts. I "re-appeared" but remained a political prisoner for two and a half more years. I could see my daughter, and I knew that my husband had also survived.

I never discovered why the military had spared my life. My parents, who knocked at every door looking for me, might have knocked at the correct door. Yet it is also true that some of the most influential people in the country were not able to rescue their own children. My degree of involvement was not the reason for my luck either. People who participated less in politics did not survive. We were hostages and, as such, our lives were disposed of according to the needs of our captors.

While I was imprisoned, no charges were brought against me. Like the majority of the 7,000 political prisoners, I was held indefinitely and considered to be a threat to national security. It is estimated that over 30,000 people "disappeared" to detention centers like the Little School. Among them were over 400 children who were either kidnapped with their parents or—like Graciela's baby—born in captivity. All but a few of the disappeared still remain unaccounted for.

Human rights groups launched an international campaign denouncing the repression in Argentina. One of these was the Mothers of Plaza de Mayo movement, an organization of mothers of disappeared people that demanded answers from the government on the whereabouts of their children. These women soon became targets of repression, and several members disappeared.

Domestic and international pressure forced the junta to free a number of political prisoners. In 1979, after the Organization of American States sent a fact finding mission to Argentina, I was released and forced to leave the country. President Carter's human rights policy had also helped. Since some of us were granted U.S. visas and refugee status, the junta knew the United States wanted the release of prisoners.

By Christmas, 1979, I was taken directly from jail to the airport, where I was reunited with my daughter. Some hours

16

later we flew to the United States. My husband had come two months before.

A short time after my arrival, I started to work on behalf of the remaining prisoners and the disappeared ones. I soon learned more about the widespread use of disappearance as a tool for repression in Latin America. As a survivor, I felt my duty was to help those suffering injustice.

By the middle of 1983 the dictatorship collapsed. The junta could not withstand the impact of strikes, demonstrations, international pressure, a chaotic economy, and fights within the military after their defeat in the Malvinas/Falklands war. In December a democratically elected president was inaugurated.

When I went back to Argentina in the summer of 1984, lawsuits had been filed against those who had taken part in the bloody repression. Hundreds of unidentified corpses were being exhumed, most of them with signs of torture. The Little School had been leveled, but the site was identified through information provided by several survivors, including myself. I testified before the judge temporarily assigned to the case of the Little School. I also testified before the Commission (CONADEP)* appointed to investigate disappearance. Despite overwhelming evidence, one year later only two military leaders, General Jorge Videla and Admiral Emilio Massera, have been given life sentences for their part in the disappearance of almost 30,000 people. Only three others have been convicted, and four military leaders were acquitted of all charges. The rest of the criminals enjoy freedom. It is true that a very important trial has taken place against the generals who presided over the country, the men responsible for the massive assassinations. But it is also true that not until justice

*Argentine Commission for the Investigation of Disappearances

is brought in cases like that of the Little School will there be a safeguard against the recurrence of these crimes in the future.

This past summer I met Adrianita, the daughter of Graciela and Raul. When her grandparents visited the authorities to request information about their children, this girl, then four years old, furiously pounded the table and demanded: "Sir, give me back my parents and my little brother!" Adrianita calls me Aunt. I was reunited with Vasca and Graciela's mother, who told me that even though she does not have any daughters left, she still has me. The voices of my friends at the Little School grew stronger in my memory. By publishing these stories I feel those voices will not pass unheard. I asked my mother, who is an artist, to illustrate this book. Her suffering during the years of repression has given her the tools to show this terrible reality in her powerful drawings.

Today, while sharing this part of my experience, I pay tribute to a generation of Argentines lost in an attempt to bring social change and justice. I also pay tribute to the victims of repression in Latin America. I knew just one Little School, but throughout our continent there are many "schools" whose professors use the lessons of torture and humiliation to teach us to lose the memories of ourselves. Beware: in little schools the boundaries between story and history are so subtle that even I can hardly find them.

Washington D.C.
December, 1985

Raquel Partnoy
85

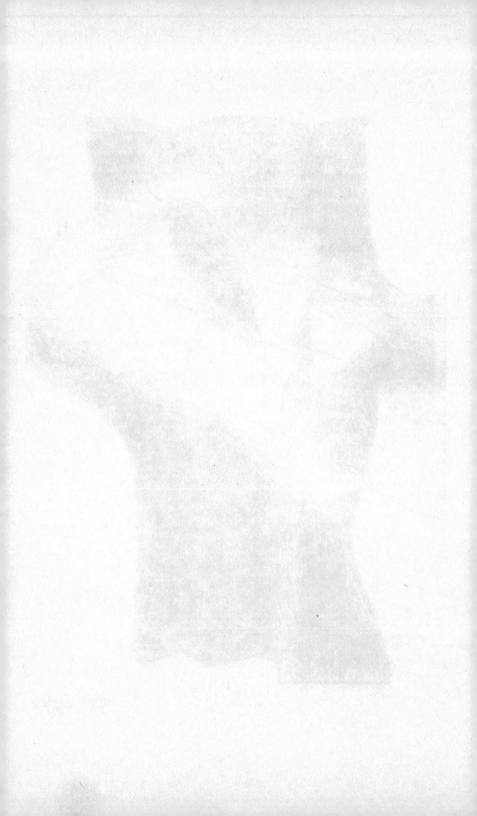

The Little School

...There is also talk of 'disappeared' persons who are still held under arrest by the Argentine government in unknown places of our country. All of this is nothing but a falsehood stated with political purposes, since there are neither secret detention places in the Republic nor persons in clandestine detention in any penal institution.

Excerpt from the *Final Document of the Military Junta on the War Against Subversion and Terrorism*, April, 1983.

The One-Flower Slippers

That day, at noon, she was wearing her husband's slippers; it was hot and she had not felt like turning the closet upside down to find her own. There were enough chores to be done in the house. When they knocked at the door, she walked down the ninety-foot corridor, *flip-flop, flip-flop.* For a second she thought that perhaps she should not open the door; they were knocking with unusual violence...but it was noon time. She had always waited for them to come at night. It felt nice to be wearing a loose house dress and his slippers after having slept so many nights with her shoes on, waiting for them.

She realized who was at the door and ran towards the backyard. She lost the first slipper in the corridor, before reaching the place where Ruth, her little girl, was standing. She lost the second slipper while leaping over the brick wall. By then the shouts and kicks at the door were brutal. Ruth burst into tears in the doorway. While squatting in the bushes, she heard the shot. She looked up and saw soldiers on every roof. She ran to the street through weeds as tall as she. Suddenly the sun stripped away her clothing; it caught her breath. When the soldiers grabbed her, forcing her into the truck, she glanced down at her feet in the dry street dust; afterward she looked up: the sky was so blue that it hurt. The neighbors heard her screams.

The floor of the truck was cool, but the tiles at Army Headquarters were still cooler. She walked that room a thousand times from one end to the other until they came to take her. Through a peep hole under her blindfold she could see her feet on the tiny black and white tiles, the stairs, the corridor. Then came the trip to the Little School.

At the concentration camp kitchen they made a list of her belongings. "What for, if you are going to steal them all?" she asked.

"A wedding ring, a watch...dress color...bra...she doesn't wear one...shoes...she doesn't have any."

"She doesn't? It doesn't matter, she won't have to walk much." Loud guffaws.

She was not paying attention to what they were saying. She did try to guess how many of them there were. When she thought the interrogation session was about to begin, they took her to a room. She walked down a tiled corridor, then an old wooden floor. After arriving at the wretched bed assigned to her, she discovered a ragged blanket. She used it to cover her feet and did not feel so helpless.

The following morning someone tapped her on the shoulder and made her stand up. Someone had re-tied her blindfold during the night. The peep hole was smaller but still big enough for her to be able to see the floor: blood on the tiles next to a spot of sky blue. They made her walk on the bloodstains; she tried not to avoid them so they would not notice that she could see.

While they opened the iron grate into the corridor, she thought for a minute of the sky blue spot. She could have sworn that it was a very familiar color, like the sky blue color of her husband's pants. It was the same sky blue of his pants; it *was* him, lying on the hall floor, wounded. Her heart shrank a little more until it was hard as a stone. "We must be tough," she thought, "otherwise they will rip us to shreds." Fear carved an enormous hole in her stomach when she stepped down onto the cement floor of the "machine" room and saw the side of the metal framed bed like those used for torture.

She does not remember exactly the day it all happened. In any event, she already knew by then something about the pace of life at the Little School. She knew, for example, that after mealtimes, if they were allowed to sit for a short while on the edge of the bed, she could, without being caught, whisper a few words out of the side of her mouth to Vasquita, who was in the bunk next to hers. She chose the words.

"Vasca," she called out.

"Yes. . ."

"They gave me some slippers with only one flower."

"At last."

"Did you understand me? Just one flower, two slippers and just one flower."

Vasca stretched her neck and lifted up her face to peek under her blindfold. The flower, a huge plastic daisy, looked up at them from the floor. The other slipper, without flower, was more like them. But that one-flowered slipper amid the dirt and fear, the screams and the torture, that flower so plastic, so unbelievable, so ridiculous, was like a stage prop, almost obscene, absurd, a joke.

Vasca smiled first and then laughed. It was a nervous and barely restrained laughter. If she were caught laughing, it was going to be very hard to explain what was so funny. Then blows would come, with or without explanations.

She shuffled the daisy around for more than a hundred days, from the latrine to the bed, from the bed to the shower. Many times she blindly searched under the bed for the daisy in between the guards' shouts and blows.

The day she was transferred to prison, someone realized that she should be wearing "more decent" shoes. They found her a pair of tennis shoes three sizes too big. The one-flowered slippers remained at the Little School, disappeared...

Latrine

'I've discovered the cure for constipation," I told María Elena one morning after peeping under my blindfold to make sure that Loro was in the other room.

"Really?"

"Yeah, just pretend that Chiche's face is inside the latrine and shitting becomes a pleasure."

"Does it work?" she asked, incredulous.

"Of course, you end up exhausted from pushing but it's worth it."

We all managed to see Chiche's face. Chiche, the shift supervisor, frequently suffered from attacks of demogoguery in which he came to visit "his" prisoners and inquired about the treatment we were receiving. All of us suffered from constipation, a result of months of immobility, inadequate food, and the lack of even a minute of privacy to empty our bowels.

In the beginning we were allowed to use the guards' indoor bathroom. Sometimes we were even granted permission to wash our hands. Then our trips to the latrine started. We went twice a day, even three times when the guards felt generous.

"Sit down and put your shoes on," Peine roared. Those of us who had shoes blindly searched under our beds for them.

"Faster! Faster!" And the rubber stick came down on somebody. The guard grasped the gauze that bound our hands and lined us up in two rows in front of the iron grate. He opened the locker and another guard took us down the corridor, one by one. We stood in front of the backyard door, waiting until the prisoner ahead of us came back. Then, a third guard took us to the outdoor latrine. Sometimes there were two guards outside: one handled the men, the other the women.

"One more step...Turn to your right. Open your legs. Walk backwards. Stop...Now, hurry up!"

"Sir, may I have some paper, please..."

I stretched out my hand, waiting for a piece of newspaper. The guard gave me something that felt like construction paper. It was sandpaper. Later I learned that sandpaper was what they almost always gave the men instead of toilet paper. I crouched above the latrine and I saw—from under my blindfold—Pato's tennis shoes. He was watching me. I also saw my dark red dress, and tried to cover my legs with it. I spotted my slipper with its plastic daisy on the dirty floor caked with urine and excrement. There was a nice breeze, and if I didn't have my nose facing into the latrine I would have breathed deeply. Birds sang and I heard the sound of a train.

"Hurry up!"

He re-tied my hands, and, again, door...corridor...iron grate.

"Lie down!" My intestines were happy then.

Some days ago Loro and Bruja came out with the "little train" idea.

"Move on, move on, hurry up!" said Bruja while madly running from one room to the other, placing everybody in line.

"Look at them. How nice! A bunch of subversives playing choo-choo train," he told Loro, who liked the game.

"Hold hands. Say *chooo-chooo*. Louder. Louder!"

I held Vasca's hand, a handshake of complicity. On my other side I felt Hugo's firm hand. Our palms conveyed a message: "Courage. For today and for the rest of the days we'll have to endure here."

Once in the backyard, Bruja still wanted to "have fun." While bringing us back from the latrine, he made us run around and around. Blindfolded, hauled by the gauze that bound my hands, I still managed to forget for an instant that the situation was absurd and enjoyed the feeling of my legs running...The joy only lasted ten seconds. When María Elena fainted out of weakness, the "game" was over.

A week before, Peine had been bringing me back from the latrine. While in the backyard I noticed they were pushing a male prisoner towards me so we were forced to bump into each other.

"Slap his face. He's got bad manners. Make him pay for his bad manners," said Loro, placing my still untied hand on the other prisoner's cheek. I caressed his face.

"If you don't hit him, I'll hit you!" I gently patted my friend's face. Loro slapped me twelve times. It almost didn't hurt. I remembered that Hugo had been tortured more than I had. . .I wasn't going to hurt a pal.

Things like that always happened on the way to the latrine. The other day they pushed me over the iron grate and broke my tooth.

Once, last month, I didn't go to the latrine in the afternoon. I guess it was one of those days; I couldn't bear the situation any more. I'd slept for eighteen hours in a row, just waking up for lunch. I wanted to continue sleeping. I couldn't stand the guards' hands molesting me when I walked by, hands I couldn't dodge for fear they would know that my loose blindfold allowed me to see. Well, the fact is, I didn't go to the latrine; I kept sleeping. And that night—while I was dreaming of a clean light blue toilet—I woke up wetting my bed.

I'd rather not think of the latrine right now. I've been needing to go there for the past two hours. . .There are still three more hours to wait.

Alas for our generation!
It is this passion
that drifts and shipwrecks us on dry land
It is
a whirlwind and, perhaps, a seed-bed.

Luis Paredes

Birthday

They didn't bring me the soda that the fat visitor promised, but just because today is my birthday, they let me sit down on my bunk bed. The visitor came yesterday for the second time. He walked around, made a good display of civility and asked us what foods we were craving. I thought he was important because of the way he treated Turco, the shift supervisor, so I told him I was dying for a soda. He promised he would order the guards to bring me one today to celebrate my birthday. I thought he was going to deliver it, and that is why, since yesterday, I've been playing with the sensations of having bubbles in my mouth, sweet bubbles. Mentally, I drank that soda about fifteen times.

I was surprised that they allowed me to sit down because, according to Turco, this room is used to keep those of us with a record of bad behavior, those who have refused to collaborate. When this farce of different privileges started,

I talked to Patichoti:

"The prisoners in the other room are allowed to remain seated after meals. They have also been allowed to take 'sunbaths.' Today it happened. This morning the guards took them to the backyard for about five minutes."

"I don't sell my friends for five minutes of sunshine...not even for all the sunshine of the world."

"Look, but there are many prisoners in the other room who have not collaborated. What do the military think they will get from granting privileges?"

"They think they'll break us." Patichoti was categorical.

Now Patichoti is trying to make me laugh. He's in the bed in front of mine, the one by the door; that is why the guards can't watch him when, bending his neck backwards, he peeps at me from under his blindfold. He has a muscular body, a great sense of humor, and his name is tattooed on his right arm. Patichoti is missing a leg. I'm sitting on the top bunk, my legs hanging down. He lets me know that he's been left breathless at the wonderful sight of my ankles that swing five feet from the floor. He remains in that uncomfortable position, his neck in a bridge, while gesticulating his delight with his mouth, the only part of his face the blindfold leaves uncovered. This time I don't laugh.

"What's wrong, Skinny," he asks, worried. He knows I'm peering at him. My seat on the top bunk broadens my field of vision. Suddenly, I confirm a suspicion that has been bothering me for two days: I see that Eli is here, too. Yesterday, they brought Beñja and María Elena...

"Hey, Skinny, what's the matter?" Patichoti asks again.

"We are all here, all of us. What did these motherfuckers do to catch us all?"

The guard walks into the room and once more I request the promised soda. Hatred doesn't prevent me from wanting to feel the tickle of bubbles traveling down my throat.

"Later," he replies. He closes the window, even though there is still daylight, and leaves. Now he turns on the radio. I listen to music at a volume so loud that it seems to be shaking the foundation of the Little School. I realize that the music isn't part of my birthday celebration. No screams have filtered through the noise yet; that only happens between songs. I read Patichoti's lips: "Take heart," he says. I know he must be remembering his own torture session.

You know it well,
they'll come for you, for me, for all of us
God will not even be saved here,
they've murdered Him.
It's the written word.
Your name is ready,
trembling on a piece of paper...

Blas de Otero

My Names

Last time I heard my full name it was at Army headquarters, the evening of the day I was kidnapped. The military man repeated it in a calm and even joyful voice. Meanwhile I could hear the sound of a typewriter in the room. It was the first time I was wearing my blindfold.

"Name?"

"Alicia Partnoy."

"Age?"

"Twenty-one years old."

"Alias?"

"None."

The truth was that, while doing political work, I seldom used my real name. The day Graciela, Zulma's sister, was arrested we all changed our aliases. In my particular case it was not necessary because Graciela knew my name, my parents' address, my history. If she spoke under torture, no change of nicknames would have saved me. But she did not speak. Zulma says that Chamamé told her Graciela had been heavily tortured. But she did not speak.

I left my house for some days, just as a precaution. I named myself Rosa. Sometimes the whole affair of the alias seemed ridiculous. Giving it some thought I decided the aliases were probably okay in a little town, where everybody knows everybody else, where there is just one Gumersindo, one Pascual...but how do you find an Alicia in a city of hundreds of Alicias, a Carlos among thousands? We learned slowly. Each pebble of information helped create the avalanche that would crush the rest of our friends: the color of the hair, the inflection of the voice, the texture of the hands, the name, the nickname...details. By the time of my own avalanche, I was Rosa. When they came to arrest me, I didn't know whether they were coming for Rosa or Alicia, but it was for me that they came.

At the Little School I don't have a last name. Only Vasca calls me by my name. The guards have repeatedly said that numbers will be used to call us, but so far that has been just a threat.

The day we took our third shower—I had already been here for almost two months—a guard was bringing me back from the bathroom; my long hair was wet under the white blindfold, my dress still torn from the leap over the backyard wall, my hands tied, my bones sticking out of my cheeks and elbows...I suddenly heard a guard singing a folk tune:

"Should treacherous Death
harness me to her hitching post
please use two horse whips to make me

a cross for my headboard.
Should treacherous Death. . ."

Since that moment they have called me Death. Maybe
that is why every day, when I wake up, I say to myself that
I, Alicia Partnoy, am still alive.

Benja's First Night

They gave us quince jam and cheese today, a small piece. I saved the cheese: there were too many good things together. I'd been dreaming of something sweet for so many days! But not this way...When the guards give us a "treat" they say it is to "celebrate" the capture of new prisoners. There was also music today, the radio blasting, to screen the cries. Now Benja is standing by my bunk bed. The guard has tied his hands to the end of my bed. I remember his untied hands setting free all those leaflets on the streets of Bahía Blanca, his easy laughter and childish face, his deeply furrowed brow when we discussed politics. We called him Benja because, like the Benjamin of Biblical story, he was the youngest of the group. We never got to know each other very well, a few meetings...I think the two of us once wrote together on a wall: "Down with the military killers. We shall overcome!"

This afternoon when they took us to the latrine, I overheard a guard say, "Hang them upside down." It must have been the torture well where they dunk prisoners in putrid water for hours on end...Poor little Benja! Now he looks so helpless, naked, his ribs sticking out. I'm sure he's hungry. He must have already been standing at the foot of my bed for over an hour. It's midnight now. By stretching my feet I can touch his frozen hands...I wish I could protect him. Just a kid! The guard has already entered the room twice to torment Benja, saying he is bored and wants to "box a little."

I have some cheese and a small end of bread saved for tomorrow...If I cut them into little pieces, then put them between my toes, I can pass the bread and cheese to Benja. The blanket is covering my feet; the guard won't see me. It's too bad I didn't save the quince jam! I cautiously stretch my leg to reach his hands; he bends his head over his tied hands and chews carefully. I've already told him there isn't any more.

"Sir," Vasca calls, "Sir..."
Abuelo strides into the room.
"Can I have some water?"
He leaves and comes back with the water jug.
"Sir," Benja calls out, "Can I have some water?" My bed shakes and I hear a strangled moan.
"Do you want water? Take this!" Another punch. I wish this coward was beating me instead. Now he leaves the room. I can smell the smoke of a cigarette he has lighted. It will last five minutes and then...The smoke is in this room...I'm sure he's coming on his tiptoes so we won't hear. My bed

shakes again and my whole body contracts in rage and impotence...Something must be done...I have to think of something to stop this. The guard feels almighty, yet for some reason I believe he's afraid: deep down he must have some memory of justice. But that's not what matters now; what really matters is that he stop beating Benja...

The break lasts a little bit longer this time. Now, I hear him coming again. Through the peep hole in my blindfold I can see his shirt: "Sir," I call out, raising my voice so he doesn't suspect I can see him.

"What do you want?" I pretend to be startled at his quick answer.

"Is there any bread left?"

"No." Patichoti, who quickly catches on, says, "Sir, I have some bread left. Can I give it to her?"

He, Patichoti, has some bread left! I can't believe it! In the morning after the change of guards, we'll do the same thing to return Patichoti's bread. Right now the main thing is to make time pass, to delay the blow...It must be 4:00 A.M.

When the guard brings me the piece of bread, I suddenly tell him, "I bet I can arm wrestle with you and win." I bend my arm, my hand open, my other arm almost glued to this one because today my wrists are tied on a short string. I wait for a slap that doesn't come. Abuelo places his elbow alongside mine and squeezes my hand. Lying on the bunk, I press my feet against the bed's iron frame. I know I have good abdominal muscles and that will help me. As tense as an arrow, I clench my teeth in yet another last effort...I've won! This dude can't believe it either, and he wants to try again...

The second round was hard for him, but he's easily won the third. It seems that he's already bored and doesn't want to take a fourth chance. My arm is rather sore—a month has gone by without physical activity. But... What's he doing now? He's leaving. Let's see for how long.

An hour has passed. The guard approaches my bed again, and, luckily, starts boasting: "You thought you were going to win!"

"Let's have a return match!"

He accepts; the motherfucker's tired of boxing. Damn him, why doesn't he fall asleep like Pato, who guzzles down a lot of booze and drops dead? But this one... Two more rounds of wrestling. I can't feel my arm but I don't care... Well! He's won the third one. He's leaving now. Outside, I can hear the sounds of the early morning, the roosters and cows on a nearby farm. Peine brings Abuelo some coffee. They chat for a few minutes and now Abuelo is coming back. For God's sake! How long is this going to last? The guard screams to Benja: "Stand properly!" He unties Benja's hands and makes him lie on the bottom bed. While I take a deep breath, I can almost hear my friend's bones pushing one another, finding their places in his body.

The guard goes to the iron grate and shakes it. He shouts: "Corridor." The door opens and closes immediately. The guards switch posts. It's 7:00 A.M.; a new day has just begun at the Little School.

48

Telepathy

Whether it was for better or worse that telepathy didn't work, I still can't tell. I tried it several times. My main goal was to get in touch with my family. However, it could have had unlimited applications. The first time I tried it was the day we ate a slice of meat and a potato for supper. The dish, an exquisite combination that deserved a better setting, slid down my digestive tract with astonishing speed. So it was probably hunger that triggered my curiosity for the extrasensory world. I started by relaxing my muscles. I thought that my mind, relieved of its weight, would travel in the direction I wanted. But the experiment failed. I was expecting that my psyche, lifted to the ceiling, would be able to observe my body lying on a mattress striped with red and filth. It didn't happen quite that way. Perhaps my mind's eyes were blindfolded, too.

The following day I tried again. It was in the afternoon, after I woke up alarmed because I couldn't remember where I had left my child for her nap. I opened my eyes to a blindfold that had already been there for twenty days. That reaction made me realize that at the edges of my mind I still believed I was free.

If only I could reach further. If I wanted, I could find a way to control my mind, to make it travel, escape, leave. It was an order. I received so many orders:

Sit down! Lie down! On your stomach! Hurry up! I needed to summon my brain: *Come on! Take off! Get out!* I had a mission. Anyway it was probably better that my mind didn't obey me. Had it followed my orders, I would have sent my mind to find out what my future held, and when it returned to inform me of the number of bullets it had found in my corpse, I would not have had any peace. I didn't have any peace now either, just the hope that there still remained a share of air for me to breathe in a future freedom.

I made my third attempt at telepathy this afternoon. I used another method. I tried to imagine my parents' house on Uruguay Street: my mother and her paintings in the small back room, my father making tea in the kitchen, my brother bent over a book. The sunlight. . .the trees in the backyard. "I'm okay," I repeated in my mind. "I'm alive. I'm alive. I'm still alive." Closing my eyes tightly, making a fist with my hands, gritting my teeth, I said, "I'm okay. Listen, I'm okay." My mom continued painting, daddy stirred his tea and Daniel turned one more page in his book. In the backyard the trees swayed. I didn't see any of them: it was just the imagination. They did not hear me either. My feet tickled with an urge to run away.

I guess it was at that point that I opened my eyes. Through a peep hole in my blindfold I saw Hugo's legs; Bruja had just brought him back from the shower. He was wearing a dress, to the amusement of Loro, who guffawed at the sight of Hugo trying to climb into his bunk bed. A while later they brought another prisoner dressed in a lady's nightgown. The guards said that there weren't any more pants left. I couldn't continue my telepathy exercise because of the laughter and humiliation clinging to the air like an annoying smell. In any case, I had been unable to get through.

Then I suddenly realized that for a short time I'd had the certain knowledge that one of my grandfathers had just died.

Graciela: Around the Table

F ifteen days ago this business of walking around the table began. At least it's something different to do every afternoon. I've already walked around the table eight times today. Two more steps to the edge...I feel a little dizzy...Now in the opposite direction: *one, two, three, four, five, six...one, two, three four...one, two...*

"What name did you choose, ma'am?"

What a question! As if they cared. I must admit that now they feel some sort of compassion; they no longer beat or molest me. In fact, I've just realized that for the past few days they haven't screamed at me either. Well, with this huge belly! But they weren't worried about my belly when they arrested me. The trip from Cutral-Co to Neuquén was pure hell...They knew I was pregnant. It hadn't occurred to me that they could torture me while we were traveling. They did it during the whole trip: the electric prod on my abdomen because they knew about the pregnancy...*One, two, three, four*...Each shock brought that terrible fear of miscarriage...and that pain, my pain, my baby's pain. I think it hurt more because I knew he was being hurt, because they were trying to kill him...Sometimes I think it would have been better if I had lost him.

Twelve rounds already. I wonder whether this "exercise program" is just one more sham or if they'll let me live until my child is born. And what after that? Better not to think for a while...The thirteenth time around the table. The "doctor" prescribed thirty. He may not even be a doctor. How could a doctor be an accomplice? That was a stupid thought. There can be assassins in any field.

Adrianita. I swear I won't think about her, at least until I reach the twentieth round; if I make it to the twentieth perhaps I'll be able to make it to the twenty-fifth, the thirtieth...Afterwards I'll request to be taken to the bathroom. If they take me I could even wash my hands. They've been allowing me to use their bathroom for the past month. I couldn't keep my balance at the latrine because of my weakness. When I get back I'm going to eat that little piece of bread I saved from my lunch...I'm going to make it last, as always. Maybe that will keep me busy for a while so I won't think of Adrianita: I spent all day yesterday thinking of her...I cried all day long. My little girl, where are you? If only my parents were taking care of her!

The twentieth time around this table. Somebody is asking for water. It's María Elena's voice. María Elena, so little and so strong, so determined to fight injustice: "We must do something, sister," she said. I guess she was repeating what she'd heard from Raul and me. I thought I was going to lose my mind when they brought her to the Little School. When I noticed that they suspected she was involved, I imagined a thousand ways of warning her, all of them impossible, there was no escape...That's why when they brought in Alicia, the first thing I thought was to ask her if she still had any communication with the outside world...In Hell there probably isn't any communication with the outside world either. Now the guilt feelings...one more chain, the blindfold around my eyes, the gauze around my hands...At times I would like to disappear—to truly disappear—to fly away with the wind that blows through the window, to vanish from the world. Such a heavy burden...If only Raul was here! Where have they taken him? That day, while the guard was changing my blindfold, I asked him—Viejo—if he knew anything. He said, "To the South, to another concentration camp." Vaca didn't want to talk about it. It's funny, I wanted to divorce him before they caught us. Now I'm short of breath because he's not with me. Well, at least I don't hear them torturing him...However, the gag of anguish loosened when I heard him whisper, "I'm okay, honey, don't worry." He was okay, lying on a wooden floor, getting kicked and punched day and night, he was okay... "Be strong, Graciela. Take heart. Do it for Adrianita...for the baby..."

The baby walks around this table with me, within me...Four more rounds to go. I'm already exhausted from walking, no breath left...I know this table by heart, I'd pick it out from all the tables of the world, even if I could never see it well. Thirty rounds, fifteen days...four hundred and fifty rounds...Today my blindfold is very tight and I can't even see my feet or the dress with the flowered pattern. Who was the owner of this dress? The child is moving...my love, to protect you, my dear child? Me?...so unprotected myself. If only your father were here. Perhaps you could hear his whispers, "Be strong my child, take heart...The future is yours." Your future, my child...we gave up sunshine on our skin for your future...The thirtieth round of this living death. Don't forgive them, my child. Don't forgive this table, either.

I smell the color of death.
All my cells are in agony...

Leonel Rugama

My Nose

Thanks to it, things have changed. Now I can see. But I recall that I've always detested my nose. It was not only because of my respiratory problems, my four operations, etc. I never liked its shape. Not that it is too big; it is just big enough to have made me feel uncomfortable. The Semitic curve bothered me, and whenever I looked at my profile, I pushed up the point of my nose with my index finger, in search of harmony. Obviously, I don't have that kind of problem now. I'm only allowed to look at myself in a mirror every twenty days, when they remove my blindfold at shower time; then, it's not my nose that worries me. Now I stare at my eyebrows that have grown thicker, at my eyes that look so strange, deeper...

When we were kids, my brother called me "Cyrana" after the novel Cyrano de Bergerac: *There was a man/stuck to a nose..."* I was enraged.

Some days ago I dared ask for an antihistamine. The "doctor," a gigantic fat man, plopped down by my bedside and asked how I was feeling. I told him about this allergy that frequently affects my breathing. He gave me a small round tablet.

The pieces of gauze that they bring for me to blow my nose pile up under my pillow. When my nose is stuffed up, I can't sniff the smoke of the guards' cigarettes when they furtively enter the room; nor can I smell rain, bread, my filthy blanket, or the metallic odor of fear. Advantages and disadvantages are balanced.

Living conditions at the Little School let this appendage of my face show its hidden virtue: my nose allows me to see. No, I haven't suddenly become metaphoric. Indeed, it's thanks to my nose that I can see. What happens is that its shape keeps my blindfold slightly lifted. Portions of the world parade before these small slits. Only Peine knows how to tie a blindfold well enough so it can trick my nose. Other guards just stuff in pieces of cotton and tape to block these little, illegal and dangerous windows. Meanwhile, my nose seems to grow, proudly, with every new blindfold. The reason is that, finally, my nose and I have reconciled.

Religion

Yesterday, when Abuelo caught me talking, he took me to Chiche. Chiche was sitting in the hall, pounding his horse whip on the edge of the table. He made me stand two feet from him. I could see his legs from underneath my blindfold.

"I heard you're a Jew, is that right?"

"Yes, sir."

"Okay. If you don't behave we're going to make soap out of you, understand?"

I was expecting him to whip me, but he didn't. Abuelo brought me back to my bunk bed.

Chiche's warning didn't frighten me, maybe because I'm convinced that at the Little School there isn't sufficient technology to make soap out of anybody. Perhaps I didn't take him seriously because I already knew I could be killed at any moment.

Sometimes when I'm very scared, I wish I could believe in God: the Christian God, my family's God, any God...The truth is that I would like to believe in a God that protects and rescues me from here; I don't want a God that makes me a martyr.

"If you don't believe in God, how do you find strength to risk being killed by the military?" Néstor asked one day. He, Christian to the marrow of his bones, found the tools to fight injustice in the Theology of Liberation. But Néstor isn't here today, nor his wife Mary. When I was being taken to the Little School, I was somewhat relieved by the thought that I might see them again. But when I arrived, I found out that they had already been transferred. Zorzal says that they were moved several days before our arrival.

Néstor and Mary are as dear to me as if they were my brother and sister. We followed each other's steps from our teens to the very same doors of this concentration camp: marriage, children, political activism...Their experiences were also mine, as were their beliefs, except one: they could never convince me of the existence of God. But I participated in their wedding ceremony, reading the Bible.

I remember I was also reading the Bible one night when I had sought refuge at Néstor and Mary's house after my uncle had been kidnapped. It was advisable to leave my home then. So many people had disappeared in those few days that at my friends' house we remained alert twenty-four hours a day. We thought that way we would have time to escape.

Sitting by a lamp draped with a towel so nobody could see in, I was on guard between 2 A.M. and 4 A.M. I had a blunt kitchen knife handy. When, later, three Army trucks arrived at my home, and I ended up here, I realized how naive we were in thinking we could possibly escape. At Néstor and Mary's house there were three children, three knives, and a Bible. By any stretch of the imagination we were a lost cause.

Mary and I chatted about our children, our marriages and the political work of women. Néstor liked to hear about my family traditions, my roots. . .He enjoyed listening to tales of my Cossack great-grandfather and my immigrant grandparents. He proudly referred to me as his Jewish sister.

Now that Chiche has come out with the "discovery" of my Jewishness, I realize this is the first time the subject of my race has come up here. When I was interrogated the guards didn't mention it at all. In any case it's not for being Jewish that I was brought to the Little School. Néstor and Mary weren't brought here because they are Christian either. So many priests have blessed the weapons of the military! So many rabbis thank God for the coup that has saved them from "chaos!" Whenever things like this happen, I'm convinced that God is just a pretext. . .and I instinctively reject pretexts.

Since yesterday, when Abuelo caught me talking and took me before Chiche, I haven't even tried to open my mouth. A short while ago the guards were changed; Peine is in the hall now. He hasn't found me talking yet. I can still take a chance.

"Vasca," I whisper. . .

Raquel Partnoy
85

A Conversation Under the Rain

This day had been different: the rain had made it different. Shortly after lunch it had begun to rain. The smell of damp earth made her come to grips with the fact that she was still alive. She inhaled deeply and a rare memory of freedom tickled her cheekbones. The open window let some rain in...A drop fell on her forehead, just above the blindfold, and slowly began to make its way to her heart. Her heart, hard as stone, after having shrunk to dodge anguish, finally softened. Like day-old bread soaking in water, her heart was swelling and dissolving, slowly but unavoidably...When she thought she was about to cry, she heard her window close.

The Little School was full of roof leaks; she had confirmed this while she was still in the other room, when it rained cats and dogs in January. On that day, water had fallen in buckets on the bunk beds; it had been cold. This time, on the contrary, rain was just beginning to fall. When almost as many drops had fallen as the days she had spent there, they placed cans under the leaks. The first four cans were making the sweetest music she had heard in a very long time. For a while she concentrated on figuring out the frequency of the drops: *clink... clonk ... plunkplunk ... clink ... clonkpluck ... plunk ... clink ... clonk ... plop ... plop ...* Can number one was near the back window, the one that had been boarded up. The second can was by Vasca's bed, the third was right in the center of the room, and the fourth was probably by the door frame. Suddenly she heard: *drip ... drip ... drip ...* She stretched out her hand and the drops found a place in her palm. She treasured five of them in the hollow of her hand, five little pools of freshness and life among all that dirtiness...She washed her hands. That contact with water, the first in more than twenty days, made her feel as if she was also washing away some of the bitterness that— mixed with filth—was clinging to her skin. She used the next few drops to wet her lips.

She slept a while, lulled by the sound of the rain, dreaming of *mate** and *tortas fritas*** and windows framing gray skies that could be seen without a blindfold on her eyes. It must have been about 6 P.M. when she decided to wake up. They had placed a can under the leak near her bed; she could count about eight cans but it was hard to figure out where the new ones were. She was afraid that her blindfold was loose and thought she'd better have it changed before the next shift. She began calling the guard. Shortly before supper (her blindfold replaced) she cupped her hand under the leak one more time. She remained in that position for a long time, feeling the water slip through the lines of life and death etched

mate: a bitter Argentine tea.
**tortas fritas: fried pastries usually made when it rains.*

68

in her palm. She couldn't resist temptation:

"María Elena," she called out.

"Yes. . ." the answer came back in a whisper.

"I own a leak."

"Me, too."

The leaks had multiplied after supper.

First, they moved María Elena's bed toward hers; after a while—leaks pelted her bed on all sides—they also had to move her bed. When the guard left, she called María Elena again. Happiness filled her body when she heard María Elena's voice only four feet from her head.

"We're very close."

For the first time in more than two months the guards had placed her next to someone else's bed. Both women's heads were facing in the same direction. The guard had forgotten to make them lie with their heads in opposite directions. . .perhaps it had been an intentional omission.

"Where is he?"

"I don't hear him."

"I heard him leave."

"Could we talk?"

"I guess so, we're really close, he can't hear us."

"The sound of water helps to conceal our voices. . ."

"It feels like we're paying each other a social visit."

They silently laughed, feeling comfortable in their bunk beds, and ready to enjoy some chatting. They sighed at the same time, relaxing. They laughed again. She had not been able to talk to María Elena for two days; the last time, in a rush, she had given María Elena some ideas about yoga.

"Could you sleep?"

"Yes! It was fantastic. I breathed rhythmically as you'd

told me, then I was so busy noticing the muscles of my body, relaxing them and feeling them heavily sink into the mattress that for a while I even forgot where I was."

"What about the other problem?"

"I haven't menstruated yet. I'm worried. I think I'm pregnant."

"Don't worry, wait some more. Remember that none of us are menstruating. Vasca, for example, hasn't for five months...but she isn't pregnant. I don't menstruate either, and also María Angélica...I don't know, it's as if our bodies were protecting themselves..."

"I told the 'doctor' yesterday. He said that he'll give us all injections so we become regular, but that he'll do it the day we're sent to prison."

"Did he say that? Maybe they'll send us all to prison, then. Did he say anything about Benja?"

"Pato told me that if I wanted he would bring Benja over so I can go to bed with him."

"But...what does the guard ask for in return?"

"Nothing, nothing."

"Who else is on that shift? Bruja?"

"Yes, and Loro, but they don't ask for anything either...it's 'entertainment' they want. They'll masturbate looking at us, even if we don't do anything."

"So...what do you think?"

"I don't know...I get furious when I think that those...but I love Benja so much! If only we were left alone...Last time they brought him I didn't know what to tell him."

"Well, at least you could see he was doing okay...this time you'll have to plan what to tell him and how. You don't have to think they're watching you...It'll be good for him to feel you close...at least for five minutes. Besides, there isn't any way those jerks' filth could stain us. Our bodies might stink, but we are clean inside."

María Elena smiled. "You're right...It won't stop raining; those cans...so noisy! I guess this one is already filled, the drops are splashing me."

"I think I heard they were taking the guys outside, to bathe them under the rain...and with the hoses..."

"Poor boys! It's cold out there. I guess I'm going to ask them to bring Benja, so I can tell him I'm probably pregnant."

"It's possible that they'll bring him tomorrow, isn't it?"

Silence.

"Did you hear me?"

Silence. "María Elena?" she heard María Elena clear her throat and look for her shoes under the bed. Then she knew it. She held her breath and froze, waiting. She felt a hand like a hook on her shoulder. "Get up! Put your slippers on."

Peine took her to the kitchen. He didn't say a word. It might have been eleven at night, and it was silent at the Little School. They walked through the iron grate and the wooden door. When they got there, Peine ordered the other guard: "Untie her hands."

She summoned all her defenses, blocking out any speculation about her fate. She did not indulge in self-pity. The hatred she felt for them shielded her. She waited.

"Take off your clothes."

She stood in her underwear, her head up. She waited.

"All clothes off, I told you."

She took off the rest of her clothes. She felt as if the guards did not exist, as if they were just repulsive worms that she could erase from her mind by thinking of pleasant things...like rain falling inside the cans, her conversation with María Elena. She thought the conversation had been worth it, despite the beatings that could come, despite humiliation. They tied her hands behind her back.

One by one, the drops on her skull were telling her a ridiculous story, a story that made her laugh just because she was not allowed to laugh. Those two killers had been glancing through the pages of an encyclopedia. On the Chinese history page, they had seen a drawing of the Chinese torture method "the drop of water"; puzzled to see that there still existed tortures that they had not used, they wanted to try this one to see how it worked.

Chinese torture under a roof leak! ... Black humor made her shield thicker and more protective. Drops of water sliding down her hair dampened the blindfold on her eyes. Threats and insults sliding down her shield shattered into pieces on the kitchen floor.

She thought of little María Elena. When they first met, María Elena was only fifteen. Five years older and carrying a baby in her womb, she had become motherly with the teenagers in her theatre classes. Two years later she was still feeling the need to protect María Elena, the girl who had dreamt of knitting socks for the baby and had found sweet names for it. She did not know that María Elena was involved in politics. However, she had some hints: her way of debating in class discussions, the kind of controversies that María Elena helped to stimulate. Her intuition proved correct the time they had run into each other in the street. It had been a coincidence; both of them had excuses, obviously, to take off in a hurry for their meetings.

Underneath the roof leak she was thinking of María Elena, her brand new seventeen years, her flight towards a future caught in that cage of death. Half an hour later they untied her hands.

"Put your clothes on."

She dressed very fast, as if she had suddenly become aware of her nakedness. In the corridor that led to the iron grate, Peine kicked her roughly several times. She thought he was mad because she had neither cried nor pleaded for mercy, because she had not even trembled. She thought he was upset because in spite of the blows and restraints, in spite of the filth and torture, both women had had that long and warm conversation under the rain.

I remember having said:
"One day all this will change,"
and I do not know whether that was
an invocation or an imprecation
or both...

Evita

A Puzzle

For a while now I've been trying to recall how Ruth's face looks. I can remember her big eyes, her almost non-existent little nose, the shape of her mouth. I recall the texture of her hair, the warmth of her skin. When I try to put it all together, something goes wrong. I just can't remember my daughter's face. It has been two months since I've seen her. I want to believe that she's safe.

"Vasca! Do you remember my daughter's face?" I whisper.

"What?"

"I said, do you remember my daughter's face? I can't. . ."

"Of course I do, she's so pretty."

I think I'll turn in my bed; that will help me reorder my thoughts. . .No, it doesn't work. It's funny, 'cause I can recall the things we did together, even when I'm not thinking about them all the time. Rather, I've tried not to remember too much, to avoid crying. . .but right now, I want to imagine her face, to put together the pieces of this puzzle. . .

The other day, after the big rain, the guard brought a puppy into our room. He allowed me to keep it on my bed for awhile. It was playful and sweet, like my baby. I felt so good that afternoon that I wanted to laugh. It was not like the urge to laugh that I experience when I'm nervous or when I use black humor to shield myself. It was a feeling almost close to happiness. While caressing the puppy, I thought of Ruth. Then, I didn't worry about trying to remember her face; I just wanted to reminisce about being close to her, to recall that warm tingling in my blood.

Perhaps if I tried to bring to mind some scenes when we were together. . .For example, that day while coming back from my parents: I was pushing her stroller along the street, when suddenly she looked up at the roof of a house. An immense dog was impatiently stalking back and forth. Ruth pointed to the dog with her little finger. "Meow," she said, since she was only used to watching cats climb up high. Thrilled, I kissed her; that kiss was a prize I awarded myself for such a display of wisdom by my child. I stopped the stroller to kiss her. . .but how did her face look? I can only remember her small triumphant smile.

Night is coming; somebody stepped into the room to turn on the lights. We were told that we could take a shower today, but it looks like we're out of luck. It makes me so angry. I shouldn't believe the guards' promises.

The radio is on, not very loud this time. . .playing Roberto Carlos' song again. When the newscast starts, they turn the radio off.

One morning while on the bus I heard on the radio:

"Fellow citizens, if you notice family groups traveling at odd hours of the day or night, report them to the military authorities. The number to call is. . ."

I was one of a few passengers on that early bus. It was 6:30 A.M. and I was traveling to a suburban neighborhood with my baby and two bags. For a short while I thought the driver was going to stop the vehicle and run to the nearest phone to alert the army. He just glared at my reflection in the rear view mirror. The night before some friends of mine had been kidnapped. Since they knew where I lived, I thought of moving out for a few days just to be safe. . .But I can't remember my daughter's face on that bus. I know that she was wearing the pink jacket, that I had the bag with stripes, the same one my mom used to take to the beach. I have perfect recall of every item in the bag. . .but I try so hard and I still can't remember my daughter's face. I could describe her toys, her clothes. . .If only I had her picture. But again, maybe it's better this way. If I could look at a picture of her face, I would surely cry. . .and if I cry, I crumble.

Toothbrush

Five days ago Vaca, a fat, humongous individual (not Gato-Vaca, I could never see that one), brought a can of insecticide and sprayed us. After a while he entered our room again and put a gun in my mouth. "It's loaded," he said. "You're scared aren't you?" I didn't move. Maybe this is why the whole business of the toothbrushes seemed so absurd. The fact was that a few minutes later he appeared again and gave us each a toothbrush and toothpaste.

"From now on," he solemnly announced, "you'll brush your teeth once a day."

I waited with impatience. I wondered how they would conduct that ceremony. It had been more than a week since we'd touched water. The method of "dry cleaning" our hands had reached sheer perfection. We'd discovered that by wetting our hands with saliva and rubbing them, the dirt came out curled in small threads. To brush our teeth without water could be an unprecedented innovation in the Universal History of Hygiene.

I inspected the brush and toothpaste as if they were objects from another planet. That evening, after supper, the guard circulated a jar of water and a can where we could spit after rinsing. By then, I'd been able to read the label on the toothpaste: Argentine Military Labs. The following morning they just left us the brushes. It was the same morning they washed the floor with the pine-scented deodorant. Afterward, the visitor came. I saw the military boots passing close to my face, and the knees of the dark green uniform. That very evening they changed the method of brushing our teeth: After taking us to the outdoor latrine, they made us stand in the backyard in rows of four and spit. Yesterday evening I fainted out of weakness while I was waiting my turn. Today, at noon, they took away the brushes.

A while ago, Vaca entered our room and pointed a gun at my temple. I felt the cold of the metal. "It's loaded," he said. "Are you scared?"

Bread

...Give us this day our daily bread,
the one that, yesterday, you took away from us.

A Latin American's Lord's Prayer
Mario Benedetti

In this climate of overall uncertainty, bread is the only reliable thing. I mean, it is the only reliable thing besides the belief that we have always been right, that betting our blood in the fight against these killers was the only intelligent option. We don't know when it is time for screams, time for torture, or time for death, but we do know when it is time for bread. At noon we wait to hear the sound of the bread bag sweeping the floor, that smell purifying everything; we wait to touch that bread: crunchy outside, soothingly soft inside. We wait for it so we can either devour it with greed or treasure it with love. One day I was given two extra pieces of bread and an apple. I kept them under my pillow. That day I felt rich, very rich. Every now and then I lifted the edge of the pillow to breathe that vivifying mixture of scents. By the time that happened I'd already been at the Little School some three months.

In the beginning, when I was a new arrival I almost didn't eat. I passed my portion of bread to other prisoners. I did that until the fellow in the bunk on top of mine told me to stop. He told me to eat so I wouldn't lose strength. But once, when I still wasn't desperately hungry, and lying on that mattress made me unbearably impatient, I cut twenty-five little pieces of bread and made twenty-five tiny balls out of them; I played with the balls, rolling them around in my palm. Vaca passed by, and noticing such an unusual activity, he asked:

"What's that?"

"Little bread balls."

"What for?"

"To play with."

He kept silent for two minutes while he meticulously calculated the danger level of that toy.

"It's okay," he said solemnly, and left, probably convinced that I was one step closer to madness. You were wrong, Mr. Vaca.

Bread is also a means of communicating, a way of telling the person next to me: "I'm here. I care for you. I want to share the only possession I have." Sometimes it is easy to convey the message: When bread distribution is over, we ask, "Sir, is there any more?" When the guard answers that there isn't any, another prisoner will say, "Sir, I have some bread left, can I pass it to her?" If we are lucky enough, a deal can finally be made. Sometimes it is more difficult; but when hunger hits, the brain becomes sharper. The blanket on the top bed is made into a kind of stage curtain that covers the wall, and behind the curtain, pieces of bread go up and down at the will of stomachs and hearts.

When tedium mixes with hunger, and four claws of anxiety pierce the pits of our stomachs, eating a piece of bread, very slowly, fiber by fiber, is our great relief. When we feel our isolation growing, the world we seek vanishing in the shadows, to give a brother some bread is a reminder that true values are still alive. To be given some bread is to receive a comforting hug.

One day I peeked under the blindfold and saw little María Elena. I made up a silly poem for her: *María Elena/sweet and small/sitting on her bed/eating some bread/Two little tears/slide down her face/People will never learn/of María Elena/sitting on her bed/eating some bread...*

Once Pato was blind drunk and I wanted to pass some bread to Hugo, who was on the bed in front of mine. Pato refused to answer my calls. I decided to do it myself. I called Vasca.

"What?" she whispered.

"Look at me!" I got out of bed and tiptoed the four steps that separated me from Hugo's bed. I left the piece of bread by his face and went back. It was the first, and last, time I got up that way, illegally. I felt as if I was returning from an adventure, and my heart beat crazily. The operation had taken two seconds.

"But...what are you doing?" asked Vasca, half amused

and half shocked.

"If he's seen me," I replied, "he'll think it's all part of his *delirium tremens.*" We laughed, feeling like accomplices.

There are also stories about bread crumbs. When we blindly look for them on the mattress, to devour them, the tiny crumbs hide and, several days later, they are the occasion for a rare event, an event that—provided it isn't accompanied by blows with the rubber stick—can even be labeled entertainment: the "shaking" of the beds. First, we remove the crumbs from the mattress; after that we shake the blanket and, while dust and crumbs are flying around, we wave our arms as if—with blanket and all—we can take off from the ground. After that we lay the blanket on the bed, smooth any folds and put back the pillows. Under the pillow is the lunch bread. It is then time to wait until our hands are bound again, and afterwards to lie down and slowly eat that piece of bread that reminds us that our present is a result of our fight—so that bread, our daily bread, the very same bread that has been taken away from our people, will be given back because it is our right, no pleas to God needed, forever and ever. Amen.

The Small Box of Matches

A licia," called Vasca one morning while Pato was in the other room changing the prisoners' blindfolds.

"Yes. . ."

"How are you?"

"Okay, and you?"

"What about your tooth?"

"It's resting."

"How come it's resting?"

"They gave me a small box to keep it in overnight."

"Hah! You can't complain now. . ."

"Well, let's say I'm resourceful."

This small box of matches is my only belonging. Sometimes I own a piece of bread, and once I even had an apple. But this box is my only non-edible belonging. Now I keep my box under the pillow. Every so often I touch it to make sure it is still there, just because inside that little box is a piece of myself: my tooth.

When I hit my tooth against the iron grate it didn't hurt very much; it only made my lips bleed. When the dentist had originally fixed my tooth six years ago he told me, "This is going to last twenty years." To tell the truth, the tooth that broke the other day wasn't mine. The tooth, made of acrylic, with a metal point, was permanently attached to the root canal. It fell out when I was coming back from the latrine and the guards pushed me against the iron grate.

My mother locked herself in the bathroom to cry when my real tooth broke. It happened at an amusement park when I was twelve. I did not have it repaired until I turned fifteen. Then, along with that acrylic wonder that closed the embarrassing window of my mouth, came my first boyfriend, Roberto. It was in that age of perfect teeth that I started to feel it was okay to flirt, to want to be pretty. Now the acrylic wonder sleeps inside this Ranchera brand match box and I'm convinced that, with my eyes blindfolded, I deserve at least a mouthful of teeth.

Do I want to look pretty for the guard, the torturers? I hope that what really matters to me is to be whole. . .meanwhile, I'm being destroyed. To be whole is to keep my tooth, either in my mouth or inside the match box, my sole belonging. My mattress could be removed, should they find me talking, as they did to María Angélica some nights ago. They could take my bread away. But the tooth. . .it's a part of me. If the guards realized how important the tooth is for me, they would seize it.

"Your recipe doesn't work," I managed to tell María Elena the other day. Hers was an ingenious solution. She had told me to fill the hole in the tooth canal with bread and to try to stick the metal point in it. I tried several times, but the metal wouldn't stick to the bread.

The following day, after giving it much thought, I had engineered another solution. I had asked for, and finally obtained, some gauze from old blindfolds, which I wore as a belt. I took a thread out of the bandage and wound it around the metallic point, completely covering it. I realized with relief that the tooth remained secured. When I took it off some hours later, the thread smelled rotten. I discovered the smell could be prevented by removing the tooth for eating and replacing the thread several times a day. That way I added one more activity to the short list of things I did to combat boredom.

My tooth helps keep my mind busy. I must remember to take it out when the guards beat us so it doesn't pop out. Fortunately, I didn't have it in the day Bruja hit me on the head with a two-gallon tea pot. It was lunch time and he had said that I was spilling my soup. The day I fainted in the backyard, by the latrine, I had already removed my tooth at the first sign of dizziness. When I finally recovered, Chiche was slapping my face. He said it was to help me recover. It was lucky that I had pulled my tooth out in time.

I was always afraid that the tooth would slip out of my pocket, so yesterday, when I got this little match box from one of the guards, I felt more relaxed. Now, while I hold it in my hand, I peek at the familiar red letters on the blue background of the box label. *Ranchera.* The rough edge for lighting the matches tickles my fingertips. Its smell of burnt phosphorus animates me again. I remember once, when I was pregnant, I smelled something burning. I turned my apartment upside down looking for a fire. Afterwards when I sat down to continue studying, I noticed a Ranchera match box sitting on the other side of the table; the smell was coming from that.

Now Pato enters our room.

"What's that in your hand?"

"A match box."

"Give it to me! Are there any left?" His voice shows stress. I feel satisfied. It's such a small triumph that fits in this little box. I stretch my arm and he snatches the box.

"Why do you want it?" He interrogates, relieved after seeing that its empty.

"To keep my tooth in, so it doesn't get lost." Reassured, he returns the box to me.

Pato screams: "Sit down!" While he unties our hands for lunch, I put the tooth in the box. The little match box will bring me trouble. Sooner or later a guard is going to decide that the box is a dangerous object in my hands. Right now it's my only possession.

Eduardo says that on a cell wall
at the police station where he
was tortured when arrested,
someone had written:
"Take heart, my friend,
one day more is one day less."

Ruth's Father

Nobody knows where he hides/nobody's seen him at home/but we hear him all the time/Rib-bit Rib-bit Little Frog.*

Daughter, dear, my tongue hurts and I can't say *rib-bit rib-bit*; even if I could, you wouldn't hear me. This little poem soothed you when you cried; you went to sleep listening to it...I've repeated it for a whole day but I still can't sleep. *Rib-bit rib-bit he sings on the roof...* I won't see you again...The electric prods on my genitals...Trapped, like the little frog...*but we hear him all the time.* I told the torturers if they took me to the meeting place I would point to him; then, when I saw him I didn't do what I'd promised. Afterward, the electric prod again, and the blows...harder: "Where is he?" But my child...*Rib-bit rib- bit...*Where are you, my little girl?

*Rib-bit Rib-bit Little Frog/El Sapito Glo-glo-glo is a popular children's poem in Argentina.

"I don't know where he is." The punch to my stomach and the torture bed again. Stop it...please! Like a caged animal. *We hear him all the time/Rib-bit Rib-bit Little Frog...* I can't turn around; my kidneys are mangled. Today, I saw blood in my urine... *Nobody's seen him at home/Rib-bit Rib-bit Little Frog...* If only I was a frog. I smell like I caged animal...I think I'm about to lose my mind. *Nobody knows where he hides/Rib- bit Rib-bit Little Frog...*Nobody knows, but I can't sleep...I like it when you say *rib-bit rib-bit,* my girl...say it again...If I fall asleep I won't ache for awhile. But when they come for me, to kill me next time...If I knew where he was hiding, perhaps they wouldn't hit me any more. Alone...they won't leave the little frog alone 'cause nobody knows where he hides. *Rib- bit rib-bit he sings on the roof...* No, please, I don't want them to come. I'm not an animal...Don't make me believe I'm an animal. But that's not my scream; that's an animal's scream. Leave my body in peace...I'm a froggy so my child can play with me... *Rib-bit rib-bit little girl on the roof...Nobody, nobody...* I'm thirsty—Sir...sir...water please.

"You know you can't drink water. If you drink water you'll die, sucker. See we take care of you, son of a bitch."

I guess a whole day has passed...I'm going to recite the poem to you again, my girl, the poem of the little frog...Soon you'll be two years old and you'll learn it all. *We all hear him when it rains/Rib- bit rib-bit...Nobody knows where he hides/Nobody's seen him at home/but we hear him all the time/Rib-bit rib-bit Little Frog...*

My girl, my tongue is hurting and I can't say *rib-bit rib-bit...*But this poem soothed you when you cried...I've been repeating it for a day and still I can't fall asleep...I smell like a caged animal...*Nobody knows where he hides*...nobody knows...but I can't sleep...If I could sleep I wouldn't suffer for awhile.

But when they come for me...to kill me next time...No, please don't come...I'm not an animal...don't make me believe I'm an animal...but that's not my scream...That's an animal's scream. Leave my body in peace. I'm a little frog for my daughter to play with...she'll soon be two years old and she'll learn the whole poem...*We all hear him/rib- bit rib-bit when it rains...rib-bit rib-bit...*

Form of Address

"When this is over, I won't even address God as Señor," said Vasca one morning. We could talk because Chamamé was on that shift. Maria Elena laughed her little laugh, and I thought I heard Batata smiling in his bed next to mine.

"Señor," Vasca called out, and we all held our laughter, "could you replace my blindfold, please?"

I heard the word for the first time the night I was brought to the Little School. I say for the first time because it can't be the same word I knew. It's not the word I used when I said, "Señor, could you please tell me the time?" or "Señor Perez, could you wait a while. Señor Garcia will be with you in just a minute." It's not the same *Señor* of "Señor Gonzalo Martínez and his wife are very pleased to invite you..." or "May the grace of Señor Jesús be with all."

"Señor..." Hugo called out all afternoon, his body twisted

by terrible stomach cramps caused by an overdose of Epsom salts. His guts were calling, but no one came.

"Señor," I heard Eli's voice in the other room one day, and my blood suddenly froze. . .I didn't know she was there.

My first *Señor* choked in my throat and I had to spit it out. It was the night of my arrival and I needed to call the guard because I wanted to go to the bathroom. Viejo, who seemed to be in a good mood, explained to me that we were taken to the bathroom in the morning and that if I wanted he could bring me a can "to piss," the same one the men used. Blindfolded, in the center of that room, I listened to the almost musical sound of my urine falling on aluminum. I could hear Viejo whipping somebody in the other room.

"Señor," I called. He picked up the can.

"Walk three steps ahead," he ordered. "There is your bed." I heard him leaving the room, taking long steps and saying, "In this place nobody treats you better than I."

A few days later I called "Señor" to ask for water. The guard sat down beside my bed and put a knife to my neck to force me to kiss him. At that moment the shift supervisor knocked at the iron grate and *Señor* had to stand up and open it.

"Señor, my foot," whispered Vasca the other day. After the first two weeks I could guess her mood by the tone of her voice when she said *Señor* each morning.

"Señor," we were calling out one afternoon, convinced that the guard was right there and he wanted to catch us talking. The next thing I knew there was the sound of a gunshot by my bed; I discovered in shock that the bullet had not gone into my body. A big commotion ensued and *Señor* left the room to explain to his boss how the bullet had been fired.

"Señor," the muffled voice of María Elena came from under a blanket. It was one of the summer's hottest afternoons, and Bruja had decided that we should lie on our stomachs and cover our heads with blankets. The guards had been shifted without our noticing it. Peine, surprised at the order, allowed us to breathe after three hours of suffocation.

"Señor," a newly arrived prisoner called out in despair. He wanted to have his blindfold replaced before the guard discovered himself that it was loose and accused him of not telling. *Señor* came to beat him up.

And it was, after all, during this period that the most senior of the *Señors* was *Señor* President of the Republic Lt. General Jorge Rafael Videla.

I curse the poetry
of those who do not take sides. . .

from *Poetry is a Weapon
Loaded with Future,*
by Gabriel Zelaya

Poetry

The Prisoners' Small Room. Noontime.

The new prisoners lie stretched out on the floor; they were brought in yesterday, and they haven't been badly beaten yet. Chamamé allowed us to talk all morning long. Chamamé says that the other guards want to take it out on him because he's easy on us. He claims he let Graciela, Vasca's sister, write a letter to her family, and that he himself mailed it.

"Why don't you recite a poem. . ." the whisper rises from the floor by my bunk bed.

"Little Alicia writes poems, Daniel illustrates them," my mom said proudly. I was nine years old then. When I was a small girl I wrote poems about the plants and birds. When I turned twelve or thirteen I began writing about my sorrows.

Now, I can't even do that. I comfort myself by thinking that my reason for not writing is lack of paper and pencil. But the real reason is this anesthetic inside. When the flesh of poetry is anesthetized, it is impossible to build poems:

> Lifelong companion:
> Eyes of melted brown sugar,
> warm skin at dawn,
> I'll tell you of my deep love.

> Lifelong companion:
> together we sailed to a port,
> together we sowed an orchard
> from sunrise to sunset, from March to March.

> And I hope
> together we find the port,
> together we harvest the orchard...
> Then I'll tell you of my deep love.

Chamamé walks into our room. He tells us to lower our voices so we can't be heard from the corridor. I blow my verses and they flutter to the ground:

> With tired soles from wearing out roads,
> from leaving his pieces of skin on the rocks,
> barefoot of dreams, almost with no fate,
> with his nails dirty from yesterday's grit,
> the old pilgrim stopped when he heard Death coming
> and, inking his pen in the well's water,
> he managed to write just a few words.

Death had an overcrowded carriage that day,
yet she folded the verses and took them with her.
The old man wailed a long scream of anguish,
a cry of suffering, of blood, of pain:
'Oh, Death you have no room in your carriage,
let me have my poems or take me with them!'

"I didn't know you wrote poems," whispers Vasca.

We hear the engine of the truck, which freezes us for a few minutes. The noise is fading; the guards might be on their way to army headquarters to pick up lunch. My thoughts move from poetry to lunch, and back. I remember the poem I wrote when the Naposta stream was closed in and channeled underground. I know Vasca would like it—we used to walk along that stream together:

Our stream was killed,
torn away by its roots,
what remains is just a hole
half dirt and half mud.
The trees were riddled with shot,
and all that was green was murdered,
a thin trace of water runs
lonely in the desolate channel.
Every forest is mourning
the death of her half-brother,
who died just because he was
too much light and too much song.

The Interrogation Room. Noon time.

"Are you going to tell us who your wife wrote this for?"

His eyes infected, he tries to read from the old notebook that still has the smell of his home.

"She wrote it remembering the Naposta stream." When he talks his tongue aches from the wounds.

"Don't lie to us."

"Sir, I'm telling you the truth. She wrote the poem about that stream near our house."

"If you keep on telling lies, we'll take you to the machine."

"Sir, I'm not lying. She wrote it when they channeled the stream underground."

"Bullshit, I know that poem was written to honor some fucking guerrilla. Get the electric prod ready."

The Prisoners' Small Room. Early afternoon.

"I was furious, too, when they channeled the stream. So many times I had made love under those trees!" says the new prisoner, who is lying next to my bed.

I hear the iron grate open; out comes the metallic sound of the soup pan that a guard slides along the floor of the other room. Meanwhile, Zorzal enters our room to untie our hands so we can eat. He discovers that the other new prisoner has a loose blindfold, and he punches him. When I hear the muffled moan, I feel guilty. Instead of reciting poems I should have explained to the new prisoners...I should have told them that at the Little School we are beaten whenever our blindfolds are loose.

If I don't see her again,
give your daughter a kiss for me.
Make her a happy child, strong but sensitive,
and teach her to give to others...

Zulma "Vasca" Izurieta,
April 12, 1977
on the evening she was taken
to be killed.

The Denim Jacket

When I got into that denim jacket the night before yesterday, I felt really protected. It was like snuggling in my mother's arms when I was a little girl. This was the first time I felt safe since the military arrested me. Earlier that night I'd been trembling out of rage and impotence because they had taken away Benja and María Elena, Braco and Vasca. To kill them, I was sure. I felt that even my bones were frozen the night before yesterday. It was April 12th; today's the 14th and the denim jacket is still magic. But maybe there's no reason to believe in magic. After all, Vasca, who used to wear it, was taken away.

The jacket is thick, with pockets I can't put my hands in now that they're tied together.

The night before yesterday I asked for a blanket and they brought me this jacket. I immediately recognized it. I put it on and breathed deeply. The burden on my heart shattered into a thousand pieces that are still running through my blood today, a thousand drops of bitterness. I immediately recognized the jacket. While touching the thick fabric and the cold metal buttons, I recalled the times when I peeked under the blindfold to see Vasca. Then I cried again. That was the night before yesterday, after they'd taken her away. To kill her, someone had told me. The day before yesterday was April 12th. I hardly slept that night.

Yesterday morning they brought my husband in the room. They handcuffed him to the next bunk bed. They had arrested us on January 12th, three months and two days ago, and this was the first time they had ever put us in the same room. But it's not because I saw my husband that I talk about the magic of this jacket; it's rather a feeling of protection.

This is what happened: Yesterday the guards watched us very closely so we couldn't talk. They tried to trick us so they could catch us. They rattled the lock, pretending they were leaving the room, but we knew they stayed inside because we could smell cigarette smoke in the hall. Yesterday, I looked at my husband from under my blindfold; he was in what used to be Graciela's bed. Graciela has been put out in the trailer until her child is born. I watched him all day long: the dirty blue t-shirt, the arm that extended into his handcuffs, his hair very long, the white blindfold on his eyes. I cracked my knuckles and he responded by doing the same. I don't know whether I'll love him again, but yesterday we didn't talk all day long. The guards came into the room to joke...they were having fun.

"Look at them, they're on a honeymoon," Peine told Bruja.

"If he could, he would hump her brains out!" Bruja chuckled.

Meanwhile, I was caressing the denim jacket, feeling the magic of its protection. Later Chiche, the shift supervisor, dropped by. He was feeling magnanimous because he'd come to talk to his prisoners. His city accent sounded more arrogant than ever. He was also puzzled, "Why are you so sure she was killed?" (I'd been telling all the guards that I knew they were going to kill Vasca. Yesterday morning I'd been interrogated on that topic. "Well," they'd warned me, "don't ever repeat it.")

"Where did they take her?" I answered with another question. I remember the exact tone of the guard's voice when he told me, "I looked in the files. They'll take you to prison, they'll kill her." But I was not crying then.

Chiche leaned on the edge of my husband's bed.

"How did you two decide to be subversives?"

My husband said something about going to the university, where you get involved in politics.

"I went to the university myself, however. . ."

"You became a Fascist," I said. I think the denim jacket had infused me with some of Vasca's courage.

"What!?" he asked, amazed.

"I said that you became a Fascist at school." I waited for the blow but it never came. I heard, instead, a sarcastic laugh. He left the room. That was yesterday, April 13th.

Today I waited all morning for a chance to talk. I was under the impression that the vigilance had relaxed. There are only three of us left inside this building. Who knows how many remain in the trailers? When the guard left after lunch, I first heard the iron grate and then I heard the guard talking in the corridor. I waited a long time. There was no doubt that he'd gone.

"We can talk," I whispered.

"It seems so..."

"He left a little while ago."

"Did they bring our child with you?"

"No, she remained at home, crying...I shouted so the neighbors were alerted. I don't know what happened after that."

"Did they go to my parents?"

"I don't know...they went to our house and then to your job. Didn't you hear when I screamed so you could run away?"

"No, I was in the back of the store; when I realized they were there it was too late. They were armed to the teeth."

"You didn't hear either when I shouted to you at army headquarters, did you?"

"No..."

We exchanged a few words in that short while. I can't remember all that we said, but I recall he mentioned that he'd liked the meatballs I had cooked the day of our arrest...Meatballs! Our last meal in freedom, no blindfolds on our eyes...no blows...Suddenly we heard steps in the room. When had the guard come in? He was right there.

"Were you talking?"

"No, sir."

"You were talking!" screamed Peine. And they took my husband out of that room. I heard how they beat him. Afterward, the guard came and started to hit me with the rubber stick. Then, the magic power of the denim jacket came true: the blows almost didn't hurt. It was not the jacket's thick fabric, but Vasca's courage that protected me.

A Beauty Treatment

If I'm not mistaken, today is April 16th. February makes me wonder whether I'm wrong; I can't remember if this is a leap year. If so, I've been here ninety-six days.

"Take a shower and shave your legs," said Chiche. Now I'm in the bathroom, ready for my beauty treatment. To shave my legs, for what? I sit down, crossing my legs as if for a T.V. commercial: *"The best beauty parlor in town, the most effective depilatory method, at the Little School. For neat corpses and Chiche's attention—the Little School, at its new location near army headquarters—is waiting for your visit!"* I'm in a good mood, which means that I'm in the mood for black humor. I start shaving. There's almost no flesh between the hair and the bones of my leg. My thighs are the same width as my ankles. The scar on my left leg, the one I got when I jumped over the backyard wall, is itching. My feet, which haven't walked for so long, are as soft as baby feet.

Next door, in the kitchen, a T.V. set is on. The razor blade is drawing little paths on my right leg. Absurdity on top of absurdity. No, better not to dream the impossible, but...maybe they'll release me? They made Vasquita shave her legs before taking her away. Then, the thing to do would be to run, to run along the streets of Bahía Blanca. Barefoot. The one-flower slippers aren't any good for that kind of adventure. Barefoot, yes, but with my legs shaved.

"Have you finished?" Chiche shouts out.

"Yes, sir," I say and turn on the shower.

Today nobody shows up to look at me. Water makes me come back to life. Who would hide me in his house? I know these dudes are very capable of letting me go while having everything prepared for another group to kill me on the spot. When they transferred me to this place, they tried to convince me that the military had released me on the street and that they had caught me afterwards. "I might be blindfolded but I'm not stupid," I thought.

Will I ever get out? They should let me out of here soon or else the hair on my legs will start to grow back. Smiling at that thought, I turn the shower off. My eyes look back at me from the mirror. Human eyes. I feel like I haven't seen human eyes in so many years. My eyes get lost in the depth of the glass. The relief of not wearing a blindfold. Who knows? Maybe someday...

There is a poster by the mirror, a drawing of a blindfolded young man. Words and quotation marks frame his head: *bombs, Montoneros, E.R.P., terrorism, drugs...* The bottom of the poster reads: *"Youngster, do not let the wrong friends misguide you or you will be sorry."* Absurdity...Now who are you to give me advice?

114

I'm putting on my dark red t-shirt when a guard comes in. He's wearing a hood that covers his face. I can't recognize his voice. New personnel are coming, I hope they take me out of here soon. Should they replace all the guards, it will be such a hard task to identify every single one again, to learn their quirks, their individual eccentricities, to distinguish each voice...He ties my blindfold rather loosely, then he binds my hands. I leave the bathroom. Door, corridor, iron grate...

"Sir, can I remain seated so my hair can dry?"

"No."

I hang my washed underwear on the back of my bed and lie down. Who would hide me in his house? People are scared and I look like a ghost...even with my legs shaved.

Raquel Partnoy
85

Outside it's April, it's nighttime.
Two fierce shadows in a fight.
Life: the power of childbirth,
Death: the sound of firearms.
Two unmeasurable shadows
are fighting inside your womb.
Life: the child is pushing out.
Death: the fear is taking over.
Do you think both these shadows could
            win this hard battle?
"Yes, they could," the echo answers,
echo of bullets just waiting
to ravage the mother's womb
as soon as the new life is born.
Outside it's April, it's nighttime.
Two fierce shadows in a fight.

Nativity

S ir, when's the doctor coming?"

The labor pains and contractions are almost constant, very close together. This child wants to get out. What will they do to me after it's born? They've said they'll transfer me to a regular prison where I'll be able to take care of the baby. I'm scared...

"Don't worry, ma'am, everything is going to be alright."
"Don't I have reason to worry, being in your hands?"

Today I was sitting in the backyard; it was a sunny day. My eyes without blindfold, looking at the garage door. Out there, just sixty feet away, freedom. How does it feel to be free? I can't even remember. And the doctor isn't coming...The sunshine, the trees, everything seemed to be so good in the backyard this morning...For a second I thought

I was on the other side of the door...The contractions are coming more frequently...The child is going to be born.

Problems, problems again. First we run out of wine, and now this fucking child. It might be 11:00 P.M. Water was put on to boil; now the big square bowl, the one we use for salad, should be washed, as well as other pans for more water. Someone has gone to get Rosa so she can wash the pans for us. It's better if I put on my hood right now. Some days ago I went into the kitchen without noticing that she was there. She saw my face. I don't like it at all that she's seen my face. I don't know whether this one will come out alive or not. Afterward, I asked her, "If you run into me once you are released, you'll surely shoot me, won't you?"

"No," she answered, "I'll buy you coffee," and she laughed. I don't believe what these characters say. On top of all this I've got a headache. I guess I had too much wine again. Well! I'd been controlling myself for almost two days, because my boss was coming to visit.

"He isn't there."

"How come he isn't there?"

"He isn't. We went to look for him, but he isn't there."

"Now what?"

"Who knows? Do you know anything about delivering babies?"

"No, but Zorzal does; he says he's helped to deliver animals in the country."

"Okay. Tell him to get ready."

"Yes, sir."

"Where's the doctor?"

"He'll probably be late, but don't worry, I know enough about these matters."

Jesús! He's pushing. . .Don't take him away. . .If only I could keep my baby inside. . .Ugh. . .Now I have to push, if I don't it hurts more. If we could survive, my child. . .If we survive. . .

A new cry makes its way through the shadows fighting above the trailer. Graciela has just given birth. A prisoner child has been born. While the killers' hands welcome him into the world, the shadow of life leaves the scene, half a winner, half a loser: on her shoulders she wears a poncho of injustice. Who knows how many children are born every day at the Little School?

Appendix:
Cases of the Disappeared
at the Little School

January–April 1977

The case of Graciela Alicia Romero de Metz and Raul Eugenio Metz:

Graciela was arrested on December 16, 1976 in Cutral Co (Neuquén) along with her husband, Raul Eugenio Metz. Heavily armed individuals broke into their home, also threatening the neighbors. Both were 24 years old at the time of their detention. They had one daughter, Adrianita, who was two or three years old; once detained, they received no news of her fate. Graciela was five months pregnant at the time, and during the transfer by truck to Neuquén she was tortured with electric shocks to her stomach and hit brutally.

Later they were both transferred to the Little School, and were already there at the time of my arrival on January 12th. Raul was forced to remain prone on the floor, hands tied behind his back. Towards the end of January he was taken, according to the guards, to Neuquén. A writ of habeas corpus was requested. His name is registered in Amnesty International's list of disappeared people.

Graciela stayed at the Little School, forced to remain

prone, blindfolded and handcuffed like the rest. In the last month of her pregnancy she was permitted "exercise"— blindfolded walks around a table, holding on to the edge. A few days before giving birth they took her to a trailer on the patio. On April 17 she had a son—normally, but without medical assistance. I persistently asked the guards to let me help her or keep her company, but they didn't allow me. She was helped by the guards. On April 23 she was removed from the Little School and I never heard of her again. She is on Amnesty International's list of disappeared people. Her son, according to the guards, was given to one of the interrogators.

The case of Zulma "Vasca" Aracelli Izurieta and her companion, César Antonio "Braco" Giordiano:

Vasca, 24 years old, and Braco, 18 years old, were detained in Córdoba around the first week of December, 1976. They were at the concentration camp La Perla and in the early days of January were transferred by a military airplane to Bahía Blanca. Chiche was the officer in charge of this operation. On April 12, 1977, after more than four months in detention they were made to bathe and put on their own clothing; the guards gave Vasca back her bracelets and told them that they would be taken to jail. I was in the same room as Vasca and María Elena Romero (who was also taken that night). The nurse came later and changed my room assignment. In my new room, I found Braco and Benja (companions of Vasca and María Elena, respectively). I listened as they were injected with anesthesia—the guards joked about it and I could hear the deep and rhythmic breathing of those who are asleep. The guards wrapped them in blankets and took them away. The next day, April 13, 1977, the two couples appeared in

124

La Nueva Provincia, the daily newspaper of Bahía Blanca, as having been killed in a "confrontation" with military forces in a house in General Cerri near Bahía Blanca.

The case of María Elena Romero and Gustavo Marcelo "Benja" Yoti:

María Elena and Benja were arrested on February 6, 1977 at their home by plainclothesmen who were heavily armed. Both were 17 years old. María Elena was Graciela Romero's sister. Both María Elena and Benja were taken from the Little School the night of April 12th and shot.

The case of Nancy Cereijo, Stella María Ianarelli, Carlos María "Batata" Ilaqua and Hugo Daniel Lovfall:

Arrested on February 2, 1977 in Bahía Blanca, Carlos and Hugo were taken by army personnel in uniform. Both were 18 years old. They were born in Punta Alta, located near Bahía Blanca. Stella María worked at the Savoy Candy Shoppe in Bahía Blanca.

Carlos and Hugo were severely tortured. Guards dislocated Carlos' shoulder during torture by hanging him by the arms in a well of water. During the afternoon of April 13, all of them were transferred, along with Elizabeth Freres and María Angélica Ferrari. When the guards took me to the bathroom that day at noon, I could see under my blindfold the feet of the six prisoners, who were seated along a narrow passageway. I never heard of them again.

The case of María Angélica Ferrari:

María was arrested at the end of January 1977 in the small town of Ingeniero White—near Bahía Blanca. She was

26 years old when she was arrested and was studying biochemistry at the National University of the South *(Universidad Nacional del Sur)*. On April 13, 1977, she was taken away from the Little School.

The case of Elizabeth Freres:

Elizabeth was arrested at the end of January 1977 in Bahía Blanca. She was 24 years old when she was arrested. She was studying biochemistry at the National University of the South. On April 13, after two and a half months at the Little School, she was taken away. On about April 16, I heard a newscast on the guards' radio, which reported the killing of two couples in a confrontation in La Plata. As the announcer began to list the names, we listened for Elizabeth's name. We heard her first name, but before hearing her last name, the guards turned off the radio.

The case of the high school students:

When I arrived at the Little School, there were approximately a dozen teenagers about 17 years old; all of them were students at the National School of Technical Education in Bahía Blanca. They had been kidnapped from their homes in the presence of their parents, in the second half of December 1976. Some stayed at the Little School for one month. There they were beaten harshly and had to lie on the floor with their hands tied behind their backs. At least two were tortured with electric shocks. An incident in which they disobeyed a professor led to their kidnapping: The students were finishing classes and there was a happy atmosphere in the school. The professor, a Navy officer, ordered the students to stop making noise. When they did not comply, he expelled the students from the school. The students' parents complained to military authorities and requested that their children be readmitted. The authorities warned them to stop complaining or "they would regret it." Some days later, heavily armed masked groups invaded the houses of the students and kidnapped them. After their incarceration at the Little School, the students were freed.

Others arrested/disappeared:
—A 50 year old woman who had a shop in Ingeniero White. She stayed for two days.
—A 26 year old man, a gardener. Guards tortured him, burning him with a blow torch. They kept him outside of the building in a trailer. He was thin, approximately 6 ft., with brown eyes and straight chestnut brown hair. He wore glasses. He was detained at the end of January, 1977.
—A young man with a deep chest wound, the result of torture. I heard him begging to have his wound dressed for several days, but, according to the guards, by the time they finally dressed the wound it had become severely infected.
—A couple who were kept outside in a trailer.
—A soldier.
—Another couple, captured on April 24, 1977.

A case subsequent to my detention in the Little School, Ana María Germani de Maisonave and Rodolfo Maisonave:
Ana María and Rodolfo arrived at the Villa Floresta prison, Bahía Blanca in August 1977 after being "disappeared" in the Little School for about fifteen days. Ana María was a biochemist and was 32 years old when she was captured. They had one daughter, only months old at the time of her capture with

her parents. She spent one day in the concentration camp and was then left on the door step of her grandparents' house. Rodolfo and Ana María were tortured. Both were condemned to 25 years in prison by a military court in a totally arbitrary and illegal manner. They were released in 1983, as a result of domestic and international pressure on the military government.

Prior to January 1977

The case of Graciela Izurieta and her friend:
Graciela Izurieta, 26 years old, sister of Zulma "Vasca" Izurieta, was captured in her home in the middle of October 1976. Graciela was three months pregnant when she "disappeared." The operation in which she was detained was carried out by uniformed soldiers. Graciela was taken from the Little School at the end of December, 1976, approximately in her fifth month of pregnancy. Her friend was working in construction. His photograph appeared in *La Nueva Provincia,* as "dead in a confrontation with the army" in front of a school. In this sham battle, José Luis Peralta also was listed as dead. According to the testimonies of prisoners, he had been detained in March in Mar del Plata and transferred to the Little School with a wound in his foot.

The case of María Eugenia González de Junquera and Néstor Junquera:
María, 22 years old, and Néstor, 25 years old, were kidnapped in their home in Bahía Blanca on November 13, 1976. The capture was carried out by heavily armed individuals, dressed in plain clothes. María and Néstor were the parents

128

of two children, Mauricio, a two year old boy, and Anahí, a few-month old girl. The babies were given to the family. Néstor worked for Dow Chemical in the construction of the petrochemical complex in Bahía Blanca. Both were tortured in The Little School and María Eugenia, who was recovering from an abortion, was in danger of dying from torture. Testimonies of people who were at the Little School before me affirmed that María Eugenia and Néstor were taken away in the middle of December 1976. Nothing more is known of them, although a writ of habeas corpus was filed.

The case of Juan Carlos Castilla and Juan Pablo Fornazari:
Juan Carlos and Juan Pablo were captured in September or October of 1976 while they were traveling in a pick-up truck on their way to Bahía Blanca. They were stopped by the police just outside the city and were taken to the Headquarters of the 5th Army Corps. According to testimonies, they endured many hours with blindfolds over their eyes, standing naked outside in bad weather and surrounded by trained watch dogs that would not allow them to move. Later they were transferred to the Little School. There they were savagely tortured: after being extremely weakened by torture with electric shock, Juan Carlos Castilla had to remain standing on his feet, while his testicles were tied to the window grating of the building. In December 1976, *La Nueva Provincia* reported that they died in a confrontation with the military. Their pick-up truck was taken by the military and used at the Little School, among other things, to go look for food, which was brought from the Headquarters of the 5th Army Corps.

The case of Manuel Tarchitzky and Zulma Matzkin:

It was reported in the newspaper that Manuel and Zulma died in a confrontation while they were traveling in a Fiat 600 on a route near Bahía Blanca. Actually Zulma and Manuel were kidnapped by military forces on different dates and in different places long before the date they were assassinated. They were brought to the Little School before the date of the phony confrontation, which was in October or November 1976.

The case of Horacio Russin:

Horacio was captured at the end of November 1976. He was 26 years old and a counselor at the Center for Adolescents in Bahía Blanca. He was captured in his home. Horacio was brutally tortured and—according to testimony—had to be transferred to a penal hospital in Sierra Chica, where he died in 1977.

The Case of "Patichoti":

Patichoti was arrested in Mar del Plata while riding on a bus. He was taken to a police station and brutally tortured. Afterward, he was taken to the Little School where he spent about four months before being transferred to a regular prison. The name "Patichoti" ("bad leg") refers to his disability; because of an amputation, which occurred prior to his arrest, he wore a wooden prosthesis. He was eventually released and lives in Argentina.

Others who passed through the Little School:

These are people who passed through the Little School and have since been freed. I will not reveal their names because

I do not want to endanger them:

—A young male student, 21 years old.

—A couple, parents of two children.

—Another couple; the woman was 28 years old, and the man 31 years old.

—Two brothers about 26 and 28 years old.

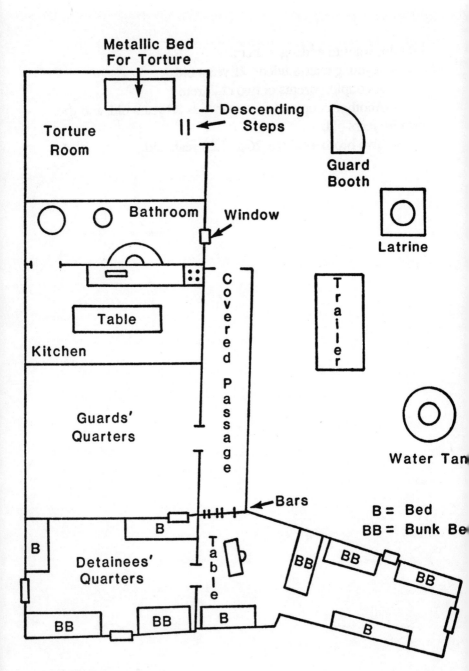

Metallic Bed
For Torture

Torture
Room

Descending
Steps

Guard
Booth

Bathroom

Window

Latrine

Table

Covered Passage

Trailer

Kitchen

Guards'
Quarters

Water Tank

Bars

B = Bed
BB = Bunk Bed

B

Detainees'
Quarters

Table

B

BB

BB

BB

B

BB

BB

B

B

132

Appendix:
Descriptions of the Guards
at the Little School

The guard at the Little School was composed largely of personnel from the Gendarme Nacional, the Army division responsible for border patrols. There were two shifts of twelve guards; each shift took custody of the disappeared people for intervals of two months. There were two permanent shift supervisors who controlled the camp every other day. These supervisors (apparently officers) were in charge of torture at the interrogations and also took part in the kidnappings and transfers. Some guards participated in the torture and kidnapping operations—which they boasted about—and received extra money and shared in the benefits of the "booty." All the guards were in charge of daily physical and psychological torture consisting of the on-going mistreatment and humiliation of the prisoners. There were two interrogators, intelligence personnel who visited without notice and apparently supervised the "work" of the shift supervisors. Every now and then special groups arrived, preceded by nervousness among the guards, who washed the floors, etc.

The guards' shifts were organized in three groups of four guards each. Each group had one working day, one day of rest (during which they were authorized to leave the premises), and one day "on call," when they were used as reinforcements as necessary. The reinforcements were in charge of picking up the food from the headquarters. Daily, the groups rotated these positions: one soldier inside the rooms, one in the hallway, one in the guard house outside, and one "rover." After months of attentive listening, I was able to figure out their numbers and how they were organized. They called each other by nicknames. Thanks to the loose blindfold, I can give approximate physical descriptions.

The guard in charge of our transfer to prison was Nuñes (alias "Monkey"), who was also in charge of the "special detainees" (political prisoners) at the prison of Villa Floresta, Bahía Blanca. The interrogators were Tío and Pelado.

Shift supervisors:

Chiche: approximately 22 or 23 years old, 6 ft., 154 lbs., straight hair, brown eyes, white complexion, regular features. In an audacious fit, he ordered me to look at him without my blindfold, so he could prove that he was not afraid of "subversives." He had a smile of self-sufficiency; his voice was slightly nasal.

Turco: 26-28 years old, 6 ft., 154 lbs., more corpulent than Chiche, curly hair, dark eyes, thick and connecting eyebrows.

First two-month shift:

Viejo ("Old Man"): Small stature, very thin, about 40 years old; boasted about working at a concentration camp in Tucumán and of working two consecutive shifts of two months each.

134

Vaca ("Cow"): Fat, medium height, about 35 years old.

Gordo-Polo: Fat, approximately 5 ft. 8 in., about 28 years old; he said he was from Neuquén.

Others: Flaco ("Skinny"), Gato-Vaca ("Cat-cow"), Indio ("Indian"), Perro ("Dog"), and five others whose aliases I cannot remember.

Second two-month shift:

Abuelo ("Grandfather"): Approximately 5 ft. 8 in., corpulent but not fat, dark eyes and a dark receding hairline. About 35 years old, from the Santa Fé province. He bragged about being a mercenary and participating in the maneuvers.

Zorzal ("Thrush"): Thirty-three years old, approximately 5 ft. 9 in., dark straight hair, brown eyes and a mustache. His mother was living in Niniguau, a small town near San Martín de los Andes. He was a Gendarme officer.

Chamamé: Approximately 6 ft., thin, 30 years old, from Corrientes, dark hair and eyes. He was at the Little School for a month, then left. Some said that he had been arrested for allegedly swindling the army.

Pato ("Duck"): Approximately 5 ft. 11 in., about forty years old, corpulent but not fat, dark hair and eyes, very dark mustache; spoke with a lisp. He said he was an electrician as well as a soldier, and talked frequently of his wife and children. He was almost always drunk. He was a Gendarme officer.

Loro ("Parrot"): Approximately 6 ft., about 18 years old, thin.

Bruja ("Witch"): Named Roberto, from Mendoza, approximately 5 ft. 11 in., twenty-ish, thin.

Peine ("Comb"): Approximately 5 ft. 9 in., about 45 years

old, dark hair and eyes, large dark mustache.

Others: Tino, Dog, and three other guards whose aliases I don't remember.

About the Author

Alicia Partnoy was born in Argentina in 1955. During her years as a political prisoner her stories and poems were smuggled out of prison and published anonymously in human rights journals. Since her arrival in the United States, she has lectured extensively at the invitation of Amnesty International, religious organizations, and universities. Alicia has presented testimony on human rights violations in Argentina to the United Nations, the Organization of American States, Amnesty International, and human rights organizations in Argentina. Her testimony was quoted in the final report of the Argentine Commission for the Investigation of Disappearance. She has translated her poems and performed them at solidarity rallies and other events, including the 1984 Sisterfire Festival in Washington D.C. Her performance is included on the *Sisterfire Album* (Redwood Records, 1985). Singer Ronnie Gilbert performs her poetry; recently her work was set to music by Sweet Honey in the Rock. Alicia works nine to five as a bilingual receptionist and is studying translation. She lives in Washington, D.C. with her companion, Antonio, and her daughter, Ruth.

CLEIS
PRESS

Cleis Press is a nine year old women's publishing company committed to publishing progressive books by women. Order from the office nearest you: *Cleis East,* PO Box 8933, Pittsburgh PA 15221 or *Cleis West,* PO Box 14684, San Francisco CA 94114. Individual orders must be prepaid. Please add 15% shipping/handling. PA and CA residents add sales tax. MasterCard and Visa orders welcome—include account number, exp. date, and signature.

Books from Cleis Press

You Can't Drown the Fire: Latin American Women Writing in Exile edited by Alicia Partnoy. ISBN: 0-939416-16-6 24.95 cloth; ISBN: 0-939416-17-4 9.95 paper.

Unholy Alliances: New Fiction by Women edited by Louise Rafkin. ISBN: 0-939416-14-X 21.95 cloth; ISBN: 0-939416-15-8 9.95 paper.

Sex Work: Writings by Women in the Sex Industry edited by Frédérique Delacoste and Priscilla Alexander. ISBN: 0-939416-10-7 24.95 cloth; ISBN: 0-939416-11-5 9.95 paper.

Different Daughters: A Book by Mothers of Lesbians edited by Louise Rafkin. ISBN: 0-939416-12-3 21.95 cloth; ISBN: 0-939416-13-1 8.95 paper.

The Little School: Tales of Disappearance & Survival in Argentina by Alicia Partnoy. ISBN: 0-939416-08-5 21.95 cloth; ISBN: 0-939416-07-7 8.95 paper.

With the Power of Each Breath: A Disabled Women's Anthology edited by Susan Browne, Debra Connors & Nanci Stern. ISBN: 0-939416-09-3 24.95 cloth; ISBN: 0-939416-06-9 9.95 paper.

Voices in the Night: Women Speaking About Incest edited by Toni A.H. McNaron & Yarrow Morgan. ISBN: 0-939416-02-6 9.95 paper.

Long Way Home: The Odyssey of a Lesbian Mother & Her Children by Jeanne Jullion. ISBN: 0-939416-05-0 8.95 paper.

The Absence of the Dead Is Their Way of Appearing by Mary Winfrey Trautmann. ISBN: 0-939416-04-2 8.95 paper.

Woman-Centered Pregnancy & Birth by the Federation of Feminist Women's Health Centers. ISBN: 0-939416-03-4 11.95 paper.

Fight Back! Feminist Resistance to Male Violence edited by Frédérique Delacoste & Felice Newman. ISBN: 0-939416-01-8 13.95 paper.

On Women Artists: Poems 1975-1980 by Alexandra Grilikhes. ISBN: 0-939416-00-X 4.95 paper.